TECHNICAL REQUIREMENTS FOR PIANO

WITH EXERCISES IN EAR TRAINING AND SIGHT READING

Book 5

Compiled and edited by Boris Berlin and Adelmo Melecci

Revised in accordance with the Grade 5 examination requirements of
The Royal Conservatory of Music

ISBN 0-88797-161-X

Royalty payments generated by the sale of this book are being donated through the generosity of the authors to support scholarships at The Royal Conservatory of Music:

Adèle Crone Scholarship   (Boris Berlin)
Adelmo Melecci Scholarship   (Adelmo Melecci)

CONTENTS

Examination Material

SCALES

Keys of A, F, and E flat major; F sharp, D, and C minor, Harmonic and Melodic.
Hands together, two octaves, ascending and descending, in eighth notes.
M.M. ♩ = 104 (Minimum speed)

A major

F major

E flat major

F sharp minor, Harmonic

F sharp minor, Melodic

D minor, Harmonic

D minor, Melodic

C minor, Harmonic

C minor, Melodic

FORMULA PATTERN SCALES

Keys of F and G major.
Hands together, in eighth notes.
M.M. ♩ = 104 (Minimum speed)

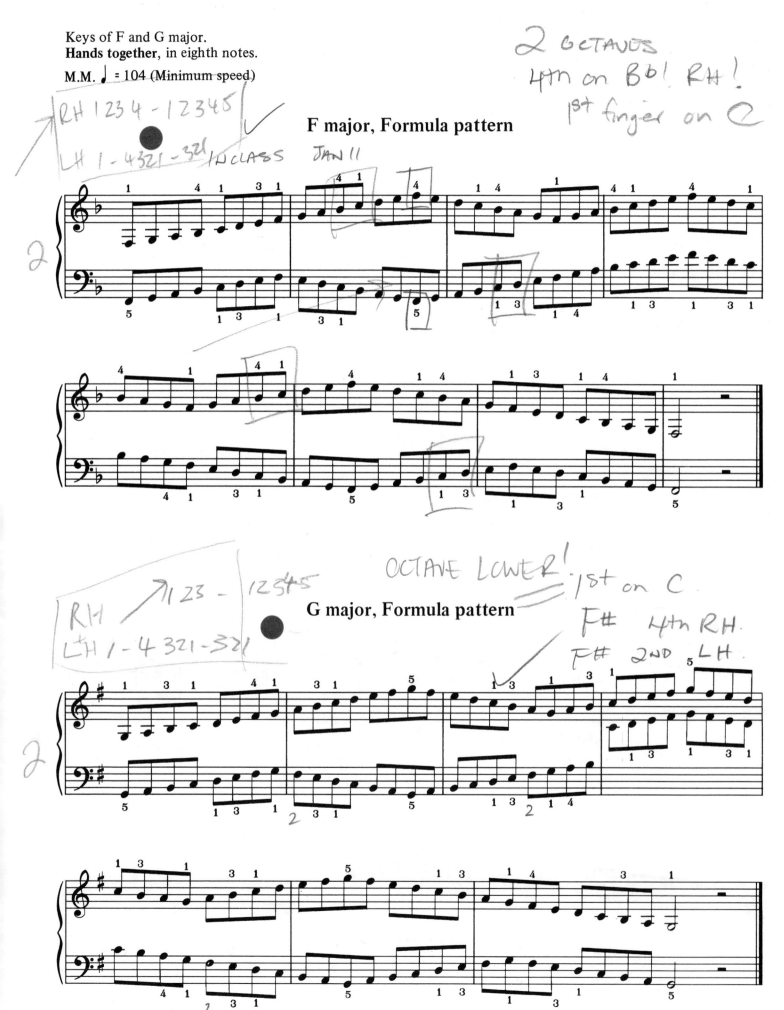

F major, Formula pattern

G major, Formula pattern

CHROMATIC SCALES*

Beginning on C and F.
Hands separately, two octaves, ascending and descending, in eighth notes.
M.M. ♩ = 104 (Minimum speed)

(handwritten: SOLID TONES BRING OUT., NO STOPPING / Pratice at ♩=104)

(handwritten box: 2ND on F & C ♩ / JAN 11 IN CLASS.)

Beginning on C

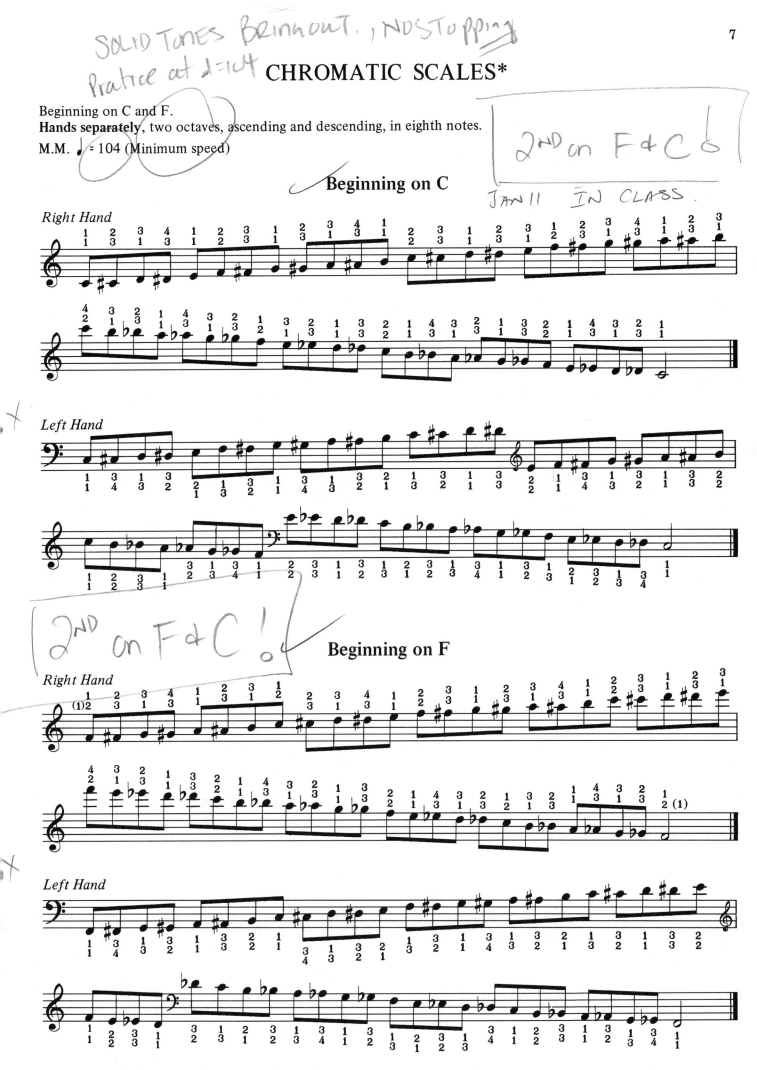

(handwritten: 2ND on F & C!)

Beginning on F

* Either of the fingerings shown may be used.

TRIADS

Keys of A, F, and E flat major; F sharp, D, and C minor.
Root position and inversions, ascending and descending.
Hands together, two octaves. (Written one octave, play two octaves.)
Solid form in quarter notes, M.M. ♩ = 126 (Minimum speed)
Broken form in triplet eighth notes, M.M. ♩ = 63 (Minimum speed)
Finish each key with a V—I cadence. (Any version of the Perfect Cadence may be used.)

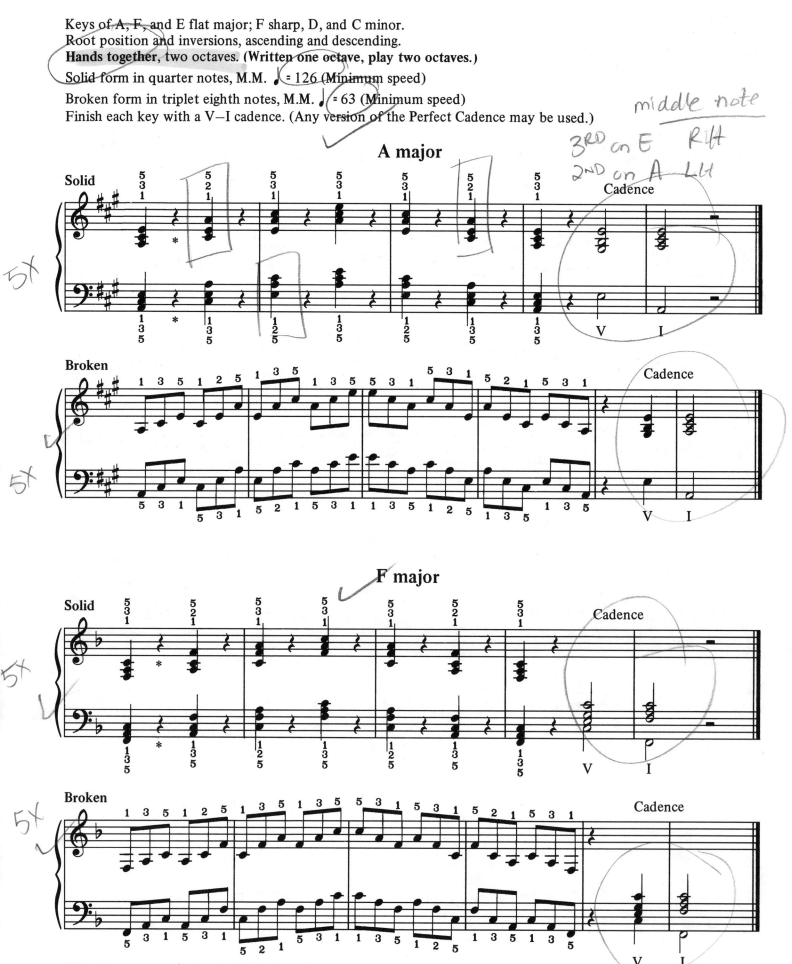

*Use the rests to prepare the following chord.

E flat major

F sharp minor

All minors raise the 7th!

D minor

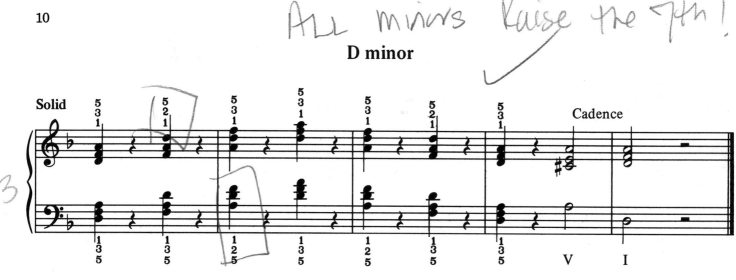

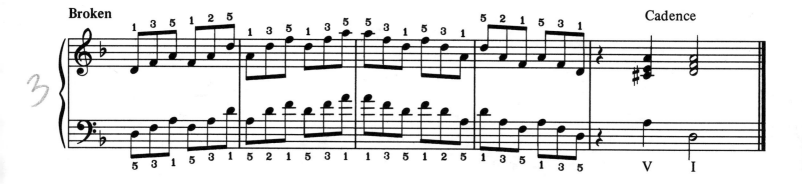

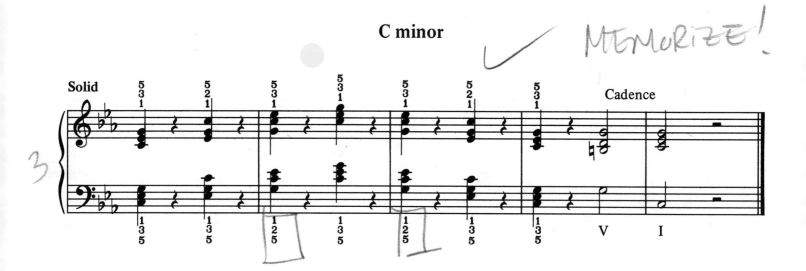

Memorize!

C minor

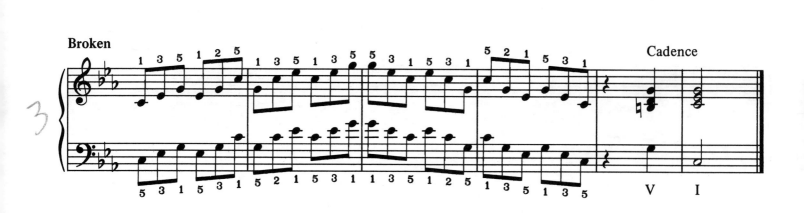

CHORDS

Dominant sevenths of A, F, and E flat.
Root position and inversions, ascending and descending.
Hands separately, one octave.

Solid form in quarter notes, M.M. ♩ = 60 (Minimum speed)
Broken form in eighth notes, M.M. ♩ = 72 (Minimum speed)

Dominant seventh of A

Dominant seventh of F

EAR TEST EXERCISES

1. The teacher or parent plays a short melody twice in three-four or six-eight time, as in the examples shown below. (The student must not look at the music.)

The student then imitates the rhythmic pattern of the melody by singing, clapping, or tapping it from memory.

The student may practise by singing, clapping, or tapping the rhythmic patterns of the examples shown below and of other tunes the teacher or parent plays.

2. The teacher or parent names a key (C, G, F, or D major), plays the tonic triad, then plays a melody of approximately 7 notes twice. The melody will begin on the tonic, mediant, or dominant, and will be based on the first 5 notes and the 8th note (upper tonic) of the scale, as in the examples shown below. (The student must see neither the music nor the keyboard.)

The student must play back the same melody from memory.

The student may practise by playing the following melodies, then singing them from memory in correct time and pitch to the syllable "lah", or to 1 (Do), 2 (Ré), 3 (Mi).

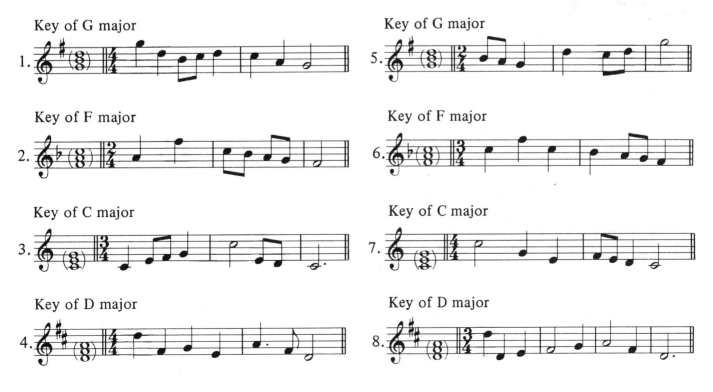

3. The teacher or parent plays a note and the student then sings or hums any of the intervals shown below; OR

The teacher or parent plays an interval in broken form, as in the examples shown below, and the student identifies the interval by ear. (The student must see neither the music nor the keyboard).

The student may practise by singing the following intervals after striking the first note, then playing the second note to test accuracy. The register of any of the intervals may be changed to suit the range of the student's voice.

EXERCISES IN SIGHT READING

No. 1

Healey Willan

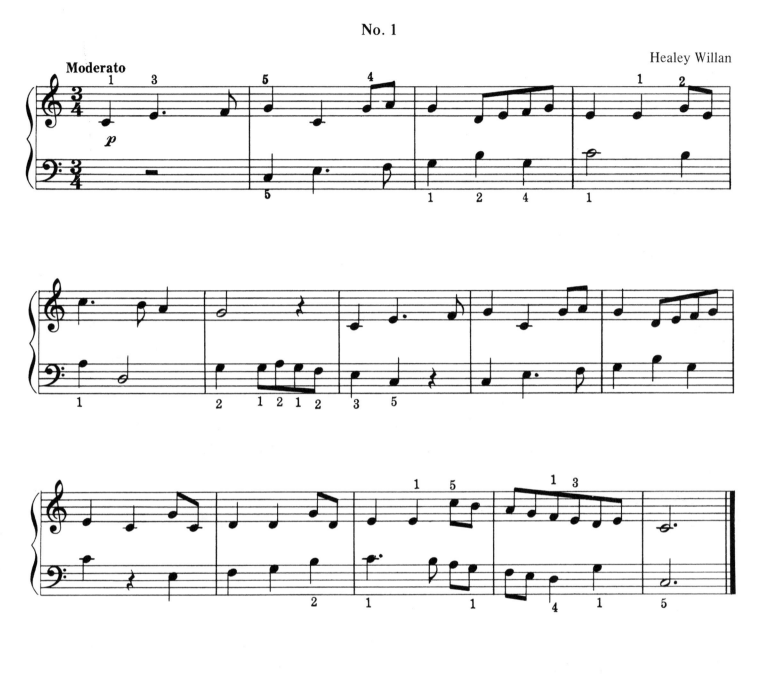

No. 2

Clap or tap the rhythm of the melody.

No. 3

Louis Applebaum

No. 4

Adelmo Melecci

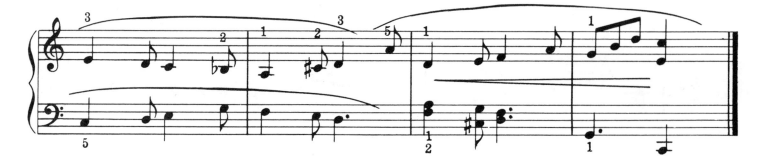

No. 5

Boris Berlin

No. 6

Johann Nepomuk Hummel

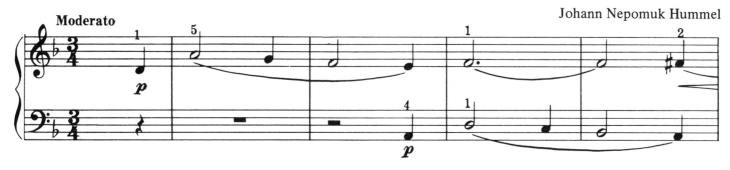

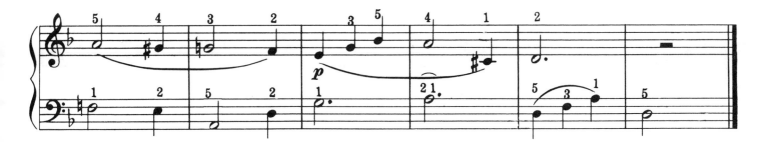

No. 7

Andante

sempre legato

Etienne-Nicolas Méhul

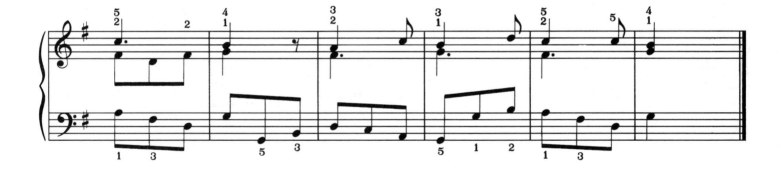

No. 8

Clap or tap the rhythm of the melody.

(a)

(b)

No. 9

Andante con moto

Ferenc Szabó

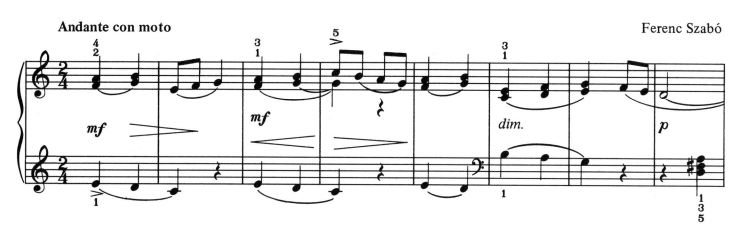

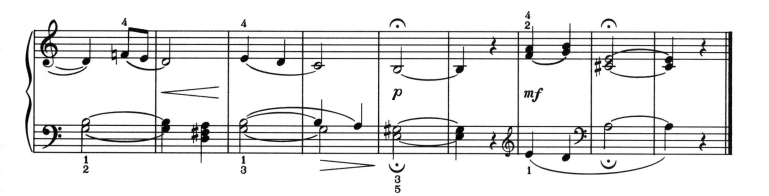

No. 10

Clap or tap the rhythm of the melody.

(a)

(b)

(c)

No. 11

Johann Nepomuk Hummel

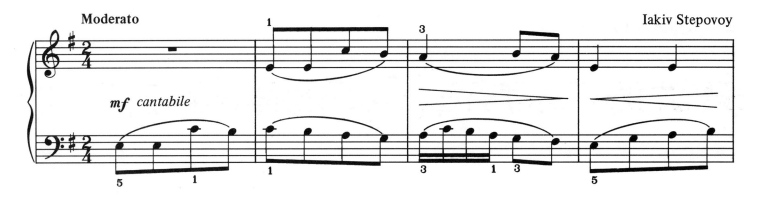

No. 12

Iakiv Stepovoy

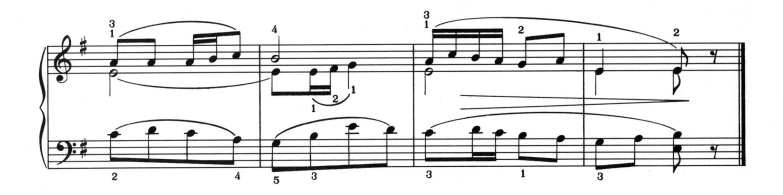